D1259610

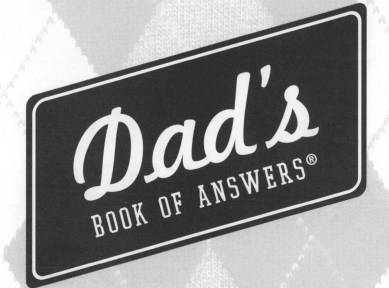

Dad's
BOOK OF ANSWERS®

Carol Bolt

Stewart, Tabori & Chang

New York

Published in 2006 by
Stewart, Tabori & Chang
115 West 18th Street
New York, NY 10011
www.abramsbooks.com

Library of Congress Cataloging-in-Publication Data is on file with the Library of Congress

ISBN: 1-58479-448-8

Graphic production by Kim Tyner
Cover and book design by Jessi Rymill

The text of this book was composed in Stymie

Printed in Singapore

BOOK OF ANSWERS is a registered trademark of Carol Bolt.

The publisher and the author of this book take no credit or responsibility for what DAD'S BOOK OF ANSWERS advises or the results thereof.

10 9 8 7 6 5 4 3 2 1

First Printing

Stewart, Tabori & Chang is a subsidiary of

LA MARTINIÈRE

How to Use **Dad's Book of Answers**®

Hold the book closed and concentrate on your question for ten or fifteen seconds. Your question can be as long or short as you like.

As you riffle the pages from back to front, ask yourself, "What would Dad say?"

When you feel the time is right, stop and open the book to the page where your thumb came to rest: There is your answer.

Repeat the process for as many questions as you have.

You will need to choose your words
more carefully

It's up to you

With a little more elbow grease,
it'll be great

How will you feel about that two weeks from now?

Don't be scared—take the first step

Build something that will last

Get the newer model

Be reasonable

Speak up about it

It may not happen overnight

Do as I say, not as I do

Follow-through will be important

What's done is done

Be courageous

There's nothing to be afraid of

Build a better foundation

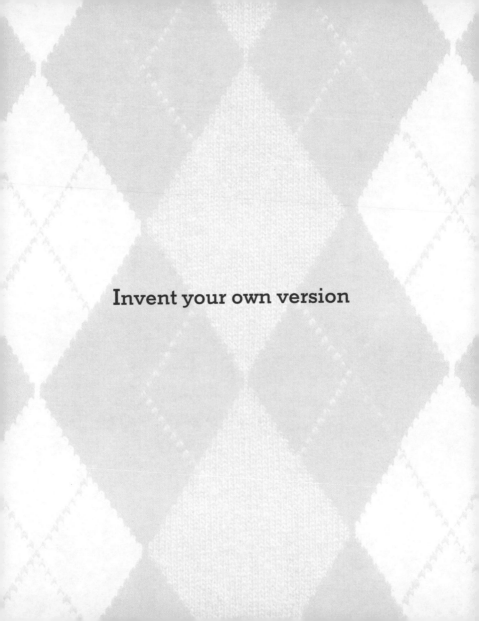

Invent your own version

Toss it around for a while until it becomes clear

You'll need to be persuasive

Study the facts before you go
any further

Take a step back to get a better look

Try again

Jump into a new challenge

The money for it won't grow on trees, you know

Don't attend every argument
you're invited to

Stop talking about it and get busy
doing it

Try to see it in a better light

Put yourself in a place where you can thrive

Consider turning this car around

It could hurt someone else more
than it could hurt you

Take care of your mother

Another day, another dollar

Leave plenty of extra time

Not trying would be the only thing you'd regret

For now, find an easy chair and take it easy

Make the call

Roll up your sleeves and dig in

Timing will be everything

Make things more stable

Carry extras

Better to be safe than sorry

Settle in for the game

Have snacks at the ready

Spend some time with a few good friends

Don't spend it all in one place

Think about it a little longer

Watch for better weather

Pay attention to someone else's strategy

Look for a better deal

You won't need any direction

Know it backwards and forwards

Prepare well for a journey

That could leave a mark

Don't let it get to you

Be focused on the goal

Lend a hand to someone in need

Get a group's consensus

Make up your own mind about it

Do as you're told

Take care of your property

Keep some spare parts on hand

Always have back-ups

Get extras—you never know, you might need 'em

Get a better picture of it

Rebuild it from scratch

Be a good teacher

Get a bigger boat

Don't get distracted—you've got places to go

You can fix that

Do your best, even though you may not feel like it

Upgrade

Be a good driver

Start off with a good joke

Make a list

Know when to stop

Get there on time—or better yet,
show up early

Focus on the big picture

Don't sell yourself short

Dress comfortably

Don't worry, it's only a little scratch

Pack light

Take your time

Go out for ice cream

Ask your mother

Don't tell your mother

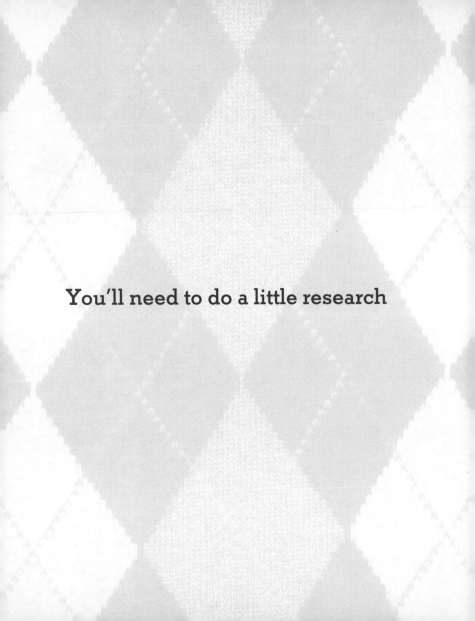

You'll need to do a little research

Aim high

Just this once

Take the risk

Be tough on the outside, soft on the inside

It's nothing that a burger and fries can't fix

Go one more time around the block

Call your mother more often;
she worries

Know how it works

Bet on the game

It would be best to change the channel

Talk is cheap

Keep your eye on the ball

Take a nap

Work hard

Invest in yourself

There's a special tool for that

Count on your Dad

Learn to fix it yourself

Keep a place that's all your own

Stand up, brush yourself off, and move on

You always look great

Get a job . . . a better job

Have a comfortable place to land

Yes

No

It depends on how fast it goes

Build a nest

Getting a little dirty never hurt anyone

Always buy the best you can afford

Make sure to check your fluids

Show your confidence even if sometimes you don't feel it

Think bigger

Know your neighborhood;
see the world

Save it for a rainy day

Always have a way to call home

Buy something nice for yourself

Listen up . . .

Count to five, ask again

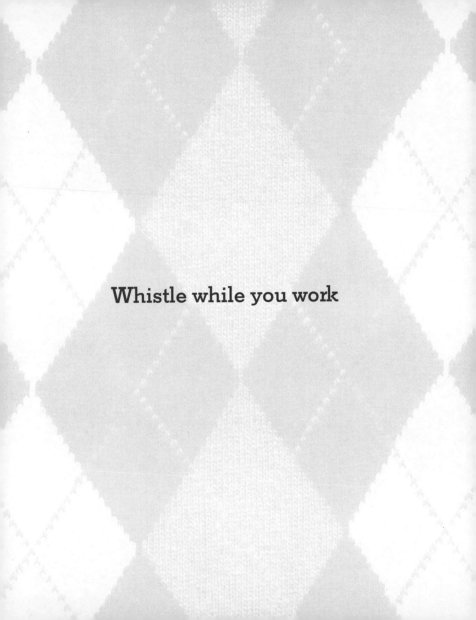

Whistle while you work

Always have some extra change

Find a way to take a break

Go play

Be rational

Plan ahead

Go faster

You can get a better deal

Check the warranty

Always have some spare change in your pocket

Strike out on your own

You need a cool drink

Endurance will be key

Have fun

Make it up as you go

Keep moving

Know when it's time to go

Fish around for a better deal

Support your favorite team

Have a back-up plan

Watch for better weather

Know your limits

Relax

Now is not the time

You'll need to finish another project first

Catch the next round

It may not be fast enough

Learn from the competition

Be a good role model

You already know how to get there

Draw a picture of it so that others
will understand

You will need to choose your words more carefully

It's up to you

With a little more elbow grease,
it'll be great

How will you feel about that two weeks from now?

Don't be scared—take the first step

Build something that will last

Get the newer model

Be reasonable

Speak up about it

It may not happen overnight

Do as I say, not as I do

Follow-through will be important

What's done is done

Be courageous

There's nothing to be afraid of

Build a better foundation

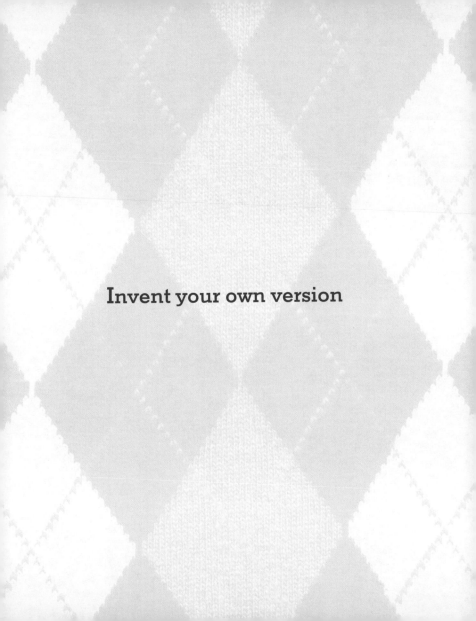

Invent your own version

Toss it around for a while until it becomes clear

You'll need to be persuasive

Study the facts before you go
any further

Take a step back to get a better look

Try again

Jump into a new challenge

The money for it won't grow on trees, you know

Don't attend every argument
you're invited to

Stop talking about it and get busy doing it

Try to see it in a better light

Put yourself in a place where you can thrive

Consider turning this car around

It could hurt someone else more
than it could hurt you

Take care of your mother

Another day, another dollar

Leave plenty of extra time

Not trying would be the only thing you'd regret

For now, find an easy chair and take it easy

Make the call

Roll up your sleeves and dig in

Timing will be everything

Make things more stable

Carry extras

Better to be safe than sorry

Settle in for the game

Have snacks at the ready

Spend some time with a few good friends

Don't spend it all in one place

Think about it a little longer

Watch for better weather

Pay attention to someone else's strategy

Look for a better deal

You won't need any direction

Know it backwards and forwards

Prepare well for a journey

That could leave a mark

Don't let it get to you

Be focused on the goal

Lend a hand to someone in need

Get a group's consensus

Make up your own mind about it

Do as you're told

Take care of your property

Keep some spare parts on hand

Always have back-ups

Get extras—you never know, you might need 'em

Get a better picture of it

Rebuild it from scratch

Be a good teacher

Get a bigger boat

Don't get distracted—you've got places to go

You can fix that

Do your best, even though you
may not feel like it

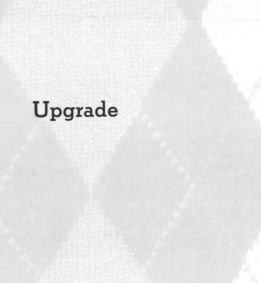

Upgrade

Be a good driver

Start off with a good joke

Make a list

Know when to stop

Get there on time—or better yet,
show up early

Focus on the big picture

Don't sell yourself short

Dress comfortably

Don't worry, it's only a little scratch

Pack light

Take your time

Go out for ice cream

Ask your mother

Don't tell your mother

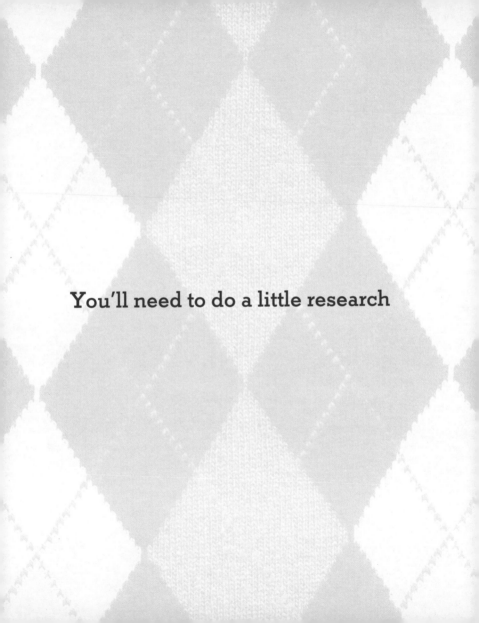

You'll need to do a little research

Aim high

Just this once

Take the risk

Be tough on the outside, soft on the inside

It's nothing that a burger and fries
can't fix

Go one more time around the block

Call your mother more often;
she worries

Know how it works

Bet on the game

It would be best to change the channel

Talk is cheap

Keep your eye on the ball

Take a nap

Work hard

Invest in yourself

There's a special tool for that

Count on your Dad

Learn to fix it yourself

Keep a place that's all your own

Stand up, brush yourself off, and move on

You always look great

Get a job . . . a better job

Have a comfortable place to land

Yes

No

It depends on how fast it goes

Build a nest

Getting a little dirty never hurt anyone

Always buy the best you can afford

Make sure to check your fluids

Show your confidence even if
sometimes you don't feel it

Think bigger

Know your neighborhood;
see the world

Save it for a rainy day

Always have a way to call home

Buy something nice for yourself

Listen up . . .

Count to five, ask again

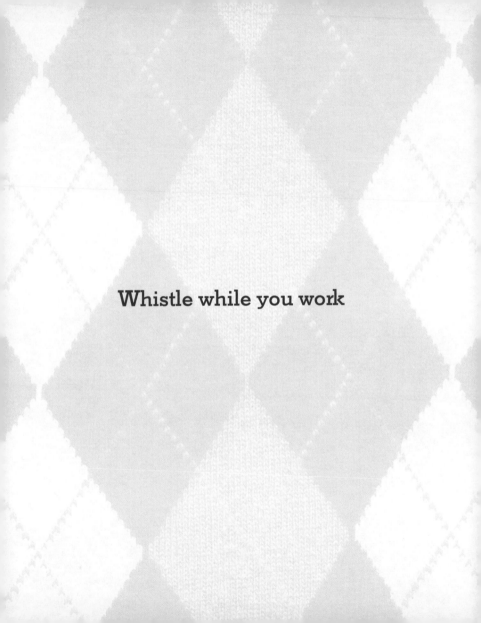

Whistle while you work

Always have some extra change

Find a way to take a break

Go play

How will you feel about that two
weeks from now?

Do as I say, not as I do

Acknowledgments

The **Dad's Book of Answers**® is dedicated to my Dad, Robert G. Bolt. Thanks Pop for all your words of wisdom, and for making sure my brothers and I had cola and chips on the weekends as well as the knowledge of how to start the mower. Like with so many dads your way isn't to share all of your wisdom in words but rather in your actions. I listened and watched for both, thank you. I love you Dad.

It is also with a great respect and appreciation that I thank my agents: Chandler Crawford and Victoria Sanders. You are great teammates.

Cheers and many pages of gratitude to my co-workers at Stewart, Tabori and Chang: Leslie Stoker, publisher; Jennifer Eiss, editor; and Jessi Rymill, book designer. I am grateful that I have the opportunity to dream up ideas and you have the skill and talent to "make it so."